Guidelines for Leading Your Congregation

MEN'S MINISTRIES
Building effective men's ministries in your church

By Kwasi Kena
The General Commission on
United Methodist Men

MEN'S MINISTRIES

Copyright © 2004 by Cokesbury

All rights reserved.
United Methodist churches and other official United Methodist bodies may reproduce up to 500 words from this publication, provided the following notice appears with the excerpted material: From *Men's Ministries: 2005–2008*. Copyright © 2004 by Cokesbury. Used by permission.

Requests for quotations exceeding 500 words should be addressed to Permissions Office, Abingdon Press, P.O. Box 801, 201 Eighth Avenue South, Nashville, TN 37202-0801 or permissions@abingdonpress.com.

This book is printed on acid-free paper.

ISBN 0-687-00110-2

All Scripture quotations unless noted otherwise are taken from the *New Revised Standard Version of the Bible,* copyright 1989, by the Division of Christian Education of the National Council of the Churches of Christ in the United States of America. Used by permission. All rights reserved.

MANUFACTURED IN THE UNITED STATES OF AMERICA

CONTENTS

Our Identity, Call, and Mission 4
GCUMM Overview 6
Purpose and Objectives of United Methodist Men 6
The Men's Ministry Specialist 9
UMMen MENistry 10
Building MENistry 11
    Checklist of Things to Do
    Some Important Guidelines
UMMen Leadership 13
    Local President
    Other Leaders
    The Nominating Committee
Guidelines for UMM Meetings 19
The Charter 20
Building Interest for Chartering 22
UMMen Charter Application 24
The EMS Program 25
UMMen Resources 26
The Society of St. Andrew, Meals for Millions, and the Hunger Relief Advocate Initiative 27
UMMen Ministry Survey 29
Resources 32
General Agency Contacts .... Inside Back Cover

The mission of the General Commission on United Methodist Men is to assist men to know Jesus Christ, to serve him, to grow spiritually and seek daily to do his will.

Our Identity, Call, and Mission

You are so important to the life of the Christian church! You have consented to be among a great and long line of people who have shared the faith and led others in the work of Jesus Christ. We have the church only because over the millennia people like you have caught the vision of God's kingdom and have claimed a place in the faith community to extend God's love to others. You have been called and have committed your unique passions, gifts, and abilities in a position of leadership, and this guide will help you understand some of the elements of that ministry and how it fits within the mission of your church and of The United Methodist Church.

"The mission of the Church is to make disciples of Jesus Christ. Local churches provide the most significant arena through which disciple-making occurs" (*The Book of Discipline of The United Methodist Church, 2004,* ¶120). The church is not only local but also global, and it is for everyone. Our church has an organizational structure through which we work, but it is a living organism as well. Each person is called to ministry by virtue of his or her baptism, and that ministry takes place in all aspects of daily life, not just within the walls of the church. Our *Book of Discipline* describes our mission to proclaim the gospel and to welcome people into the body of Christ, to lead people to a commitment to God through Jesus Christ, to nurture them in Christian living by various means of grace, and to send them into the world as agents of Jesus Christ (¶121). Thus, through you—and many other Christians—this very relational mission continues. (The *Discipline* explains the ministry of all Christians and the essence of servant ministry and leadership in ¶¶125–137.)

Essential Leadership Functions

Five functions of leadership are essential to strengthen and support the ministry of the church: identifying and supporting leaders as spiritual leaders, discovering current reality, naming shared vision, developing action plans, and monitoring the journey. This Guideline will help you identify these elements and set a course for ministry.

Lead in the Spirit

Each leader is a spiritual leader and has the opportunity to model spiritual maturity and discipline. John Wesley referred to the disciplines that cultivate a relationship with God as the "means of grace" and suggested several means: prayer, Bible study, fasting, public and private worship, Christian conversation, and acts of mercy. Local church leaders are strongly encouraged to identify their own spiritual practices, cultivate new ones as they grow in their own faith, and model and encourage these practices among their ministry team participants.

Discover Current Reality
"The way things are" is your current reality. How you organize, who does what, how bills get paid and plans get made are all building blocks of your current reality. Spend time with people who have been in this ministry and with your committee members to assess their view of how things are. Use "Christian conversation," one of the means of grace, not only to talk to others openly about their understanding of current reality but also to listen for the voice of God regarding your area of ministry.

Name Shared Vision
"The way things are" is only a prelude to "the way you want things to be." When the church is truly of God, it is the way God would envision it to be. Spend time with your committee and with other leaders in the church to discern the best and most faithful future you can imagine. How can you together identify your role and place in a faithful community that extends itself in its fourfold mission of reaching out and receiving people in the name of God, relating people to God, nurturing them in Christ and Christian living, and sending them forth as ministers into the world? Examine your committee's role and its place in that big picture and try to see yourselves as God's agents of grace and love.

Develop Action Plans
How do you get from here (your current reality) to there (your shared vision)? As a leader, one of your tasks is to hold in view both what is and what is hoped for so that you can build bridges to the future. These bridges are the interim goals and the action plans needed to accomplish the goals that will make your vision a reality. Remember that God may open up many (or different) avenues to that future, so be flexible and open to setting new goals and accepting new challenges. Action plans that describe how to meet interim goals should be specific, measurable, and attainable. While it is faithful to allow for the wondrous work of God in setting out bold plans, balance that boldness with realism. You and your committee will find information and tips here on developing and implementing the shared vision, the goals toward that vision, and the specific action plans that will accomplish the goals.

Monitor the Journey
A fifth responsibility of leaders is to keep an eye on how things are going. Setbacks will surely occur, but effective leaders keep moving toward their envisioned future. Not only will you monitor the progress of your committee's action plans to a faithful future but you will also be called to evaluate them in light of the ministry of the rest of the church. Immerse yourself and your plans in God's love and care. Voices from the congregation (both pro and con) may be the nudging of God to shift direction, rethink or plan, or move ahead boldly and without fear. Faithful leaders are attentive to the discernment of the congregation and to the heart of God in fulfilling the mission of the church.

GCUMM Overview

The mission of the General Commission on United Methodist Men (GCUMM) is to strengthen the spiritual life of men in The United Methodist Church. How does this happen? By reaching the hearts of men for Jesus Christ.

Reaching the hearts of men for Christ requires a focused strategy. In 2001, at our National Gathering (formerly called Congress), United Methodist Men agreed upon four goals:

- to help men grow spiritually
- to become partners in ministry with clergy
- to connect with young people (especially young men)
- to have an accountable male friend in Christ.

Reaching the hearts of men for Christ means engaging men through ministry and developing them as Christian disciples. This concept is reflected in the overall theme of United Methodist Men, which is to offer ministry TO men for a ministry THROUGH men.

The GCUMM develops and offers resources for men and the local church to help men develop effective ministry TO and THROUGH men.

Purpose and Objectives of United Methodist Men

The *Book of Discipline* states that: "Each church or charge shall have an organized unit of United Methodist Men chartered and annually renewed through the General Commission on United Methodist Men to provide a dedicated ministry for building men spiritually and involving men in the total ministry of the Church.

Local church resource material for supporting effective men's ministries shall be provided by the district, conference, and jurisdictional organizations of United Methodist Men and the General Commission on United Methodist Men.

United Methodist Men exists to declare the centrality of Christ in every man's life. Men's ministry leads to the spiritual growth of men and to effective discipleship. This purpose is served as men are called to model the servant leadership of Jesus Christ.

Individual and group strategies form the foundation of UMMen ministry and include the following:
- enhance Evangelism, Mission, and Spiritual Life (EMS), as men become servant leaders
- advocate programs that train men within local churches to promote specific ministries including prayer, missions, stewardship, hunger relief, and Civic/Youth Serving Ministries
- forge pastoral partnerships by men committed to the effective support and service of clergy and local congregations
- assist men in their ever-changing relationships, roles, and responsibilities in the family setting, workplace, and society

Men seeking membership in a local unit of United Methodist Men will be asked to subscribe to the major strategies listed above and to these personal objectives:
- to engage daily in Bible study and prayer
- to be a witness to Christ's way in daily work and in all personal contacts through words and action
- to engage in Christian service.

United Methodist Men may be organized in one or more components within a local church as needed. Multiple local churches may also form a single unit of United Methodist Men according to their needs. Membership shall be open to any man who indicates his desire to belong and to participate in the ministry of the church through United Methodist Men. The appointed clergy of the local church or charge shall be an ex-officio member of the unit and of its executive committee.

New Opportunities in Men's Ministry

The 2004 General Conference supported legislation that encourages local churches to celebrate a special Men's Ministry Sunday. This Men's Ministry Sunday may be observed annually on a Sunday designated by the local congregation. The day is to celebrate the men's ministry within and beyond the local church. This includes organized (chartered or unchartered) units of United Methodist Men, male Emmaus reunion communities, work teams, prayer groups, Bible studies, study and enrichment groups, and so forth. Resources for this observance shall be provided by the General Commission on United Methodist Men.

The 2004 General Conference also supported legislation that asks local churches to report the men's ministries conducted by its men. The men's ministry report shall include any organized units of United Methodist Men chartered and annually renewed through the General Commission on United Methodist Men and/or other organized men's ministry groups in a local United Methodist Church. These men's ministries shall report annually through the charge conference and shall be certified as a men's ministry and resourced through the General Commission on United Methodist Men.

The Men's Ministry Specialist

The notion of starting and sustaining a life-changing men's ministry can be overwhelming. Where do you begin? What first steps should you take? Who can you get to help you? By experiencing Men's Ministry Specialist training and ongoing follow-up, you will discover the answers to the above questions.

What is a Men's Ministry Specialist?
A Men's Ministry Specialist is someone who receives training to:
1. build an effective men's leadership team (MLT) at the local church level. This team is comprised of the pastor and key men in the church.
2. lead the men's leadership team (MLT) in discerning and visioning the kinds of ministries that will engage men in your local church context.
3. mobilize and develop leadership for men's ministry at all levels of the United Methodist Church.

What Happens at a Men's Ministry Specialist Training Event?
The General Commission on United Methodist Men has a strategic alliance with Man in the Mirror Ministries. Man in the Mirror conducts the Men's Ministry Specialist training at which attendees learn how to:
1. use a Men's Ministry Action Plan as a tool for discernment and visioning men's ministry in the local church.
2. recruit and build an MLT including the pastor and key men in the local church.
3. create momentum for men's ministry through men's events and activities.
4. capture momentum for men's ministry through follow-up activities and short-term ministry opportunities.
5. sustain momentum for men's ministry through long-term ministry planning and implementation.

This training experience is just the beginning of the support offered to a Men's Ministry Specialist. To provide ongoing support to MLT's, each Men's Ministry Specialist will be a leader in the Leadership Learning Community.

What is the Leadership Learning Community?
The Leadership Learning Community is comprised of every person who attends a Men's Ministry Specialist Training event and all persons on men's leadership teams in local churches. The Leadership Learning Community exists for the purpose of providing ongoing support, encouragement, and inspiration for Men's Leadership Teams.

Every six months the Leadership Learning Community will meet in local settings throughout the nation. These meetings will take place simultaneously so that each local Leadership Learning Community will be connected with the larger national Leadership Learning Community via video streaming.

The Leadership Learning Community will meet every six months for two reasons:
1. Face to face sharing of successes and failures in men's ministry between men's ministry specialists in your district and Annual Conference areas. This will lead to community building, networking, and group learning opportunities that are relevant for your ministry context.
2. National networking through video streaming. For 60-90 minutes Leadership Learning Communities will be able to hear and dialogue about best practices in men's ministries across the nation.

UMMen MENistry

Men's ministry is generally recognized as Christian service and outreach accomplished among, to, and through Christian men. United Methodist Men has adopted a new term defining the *men's ministry work of United Methodist Men*. **MENistry** is two or more UMMen taking actions together, serving and blessing others, and honoring Christ.

There are two types of MENistry:
- **internal MENistry:** work done TO men, equipping men for spiritual growth as servant leaders
- **external MENistry:** work done THROUGH men, serving others and honoring Christ.

As men are built spiritually from within, they are readied for good works and service to others. For this reason, UMM focuses first on the spiritual condition and heart of a man (internal) then equips men to reach out to others through evangelism, missions, and a spiritual life (external).

MENistry is developed within UMMen through two primary programs. The first is MENistry Training, which is conducted regionally for the purpose of recruiting and equipping leaders. A comprehensive training curriculum is offered for men who desire to be leaders among UMMen. This training will be delivered locally by men who are certified UMMen Trainers. At every training event, attendees who are interested in becoming trainers are identified. Resources and additional training are provided to them so that they can meet the needs of our churches at a local and district level. The second is TQuest, which is offered by GCUMM as a resource geared to promote the personal transformation of men. TQuest materials are designed to be used by men in small teams, in a Wesleyan format. In a TQuest group, four to six men journey together into their hearts with the guidance of TQuest men's spiritual formation resources. A journal is included for men to document their spiritual journey.

Building MENistry

The suggestions offered below are helpful in developing an effective men's ministry in a local church. The very first step to starting any men's ministry is prayer. Seek the guidance of the Holy Spirit in discovering the direction your men's ministry will take.

Checklist of Things to Do

- **LIST** (with the help of your pastor) the men in your church who may have an interest in reaching other men and who have good relational skills.
- **CONTACT** your district United Methodist Men's president to help you in the organization and programming of your local unit.
- **CALL** the men you identify to help you with the organization. Ask them to join you in praying and discerning the direction of the men's ministry.
- **MEET** with your leadership team and begin by developing a clear understanding of your purpose. The purpose of your men's ministry should support the overarching purpose and mission of your church. A written purpose statement is recommended. Here is a sample Men's Ministry Purpose Statement: *To reach men in our community with a credible offer of the gospel and equip them as servant leaders for their families, church, work, and community.*
- **SURVEY** the men in your church to determine their interests and needs. It is important to assess the kinds of ministries that appeal to your men. Please use the men's ministry survey on pages 29-31.
- **BASE** your men's ministry on relationships rather than on elaborate programs or tasks. The foundation of a successful men's ministry is building relationships. Events attract men, but relationships make them stick.
- **EMPHASIZE** spiritual growth. Men's groups often make the mistake of emphasizing the fellowship among men over the need for men to grow spiritually. Fellowship happens; spiritual growth must be intentional. Offer opportunities for men to grow in Christ, and expect them to participate.
- **STUDY** the job description for local presidents as you select your leadership. Energetic, visionary, ministry-oriented leaders are needed to lead any

UMM group. The job description signals to potential leaders the expectations of their leadership should they be selected to lead the local men's ministry. Leaders should be willing to fulfill the job requirements before they agree to take on the responsibility.

- **CHOOSE** a date for your first organizational meeting. This meeting should be the only business meeting held with the entire membership. Normally, the executive committee should handle business with annual reports to the membership. It is important to develop a calendar, listing all United Methodist Men's Ministry activities for the year. Coordinate the calendar with the total church programs to avoid conflicts.
- **COMPLETE** charter application on page 24. (If you have questions about the application, call the GCUMM office). Chartering is required for every organized men's group by The Book of Discipline. Completed charter applications must be sent to the General Commission on United Methodist Men. (See the section on "How to Charter," page 23).
- **RECRUIT EMS** (Every Man Shares in Evangelism, Mission, and Spiritual Life) members. It is important that every man in your church become an EMS member. It allows every man to be touched by the ministry of United Methodist Men locally, conference-wide, and nationally. Turn to page 25 to learn more about EMS.
- **DEVELOP** a strategy for your men's ministry. With the input of your pastor, the help of your district UMM president, and the vision of several men, develop your plans for the year. Men like to know what the organization is planning and where it is headed. Offer a variety of programs and ministries that your men will find interesting, stimulating, meaningful, and spirit-led. When you charter, you will receive an annual program book with ideas for your ministry program.
- **BUDGET** for your group. It is recommended that every local UMM unit develop a MENistry budget for their program. The budget should reflect the purpose and mission of your local UMM unit.

Some Important Guidelines

- Adopt a long-term / low pressure outlook. Men come along at different speeds. Give them permission to buy in at their own pace. Be persistent but not pushy. Don't expect more from men than they can, or will, realistically give.

- Don't be angry with men because they are not more committed. It is easy to become impatient with men who are not ready to make commitments to our groups. We get frustrated or angry with men because they are not more involved. This is a marathon not a sprint. We must be in this for the long haul. Continue to show men Christ, develop dynamic programs and ministries, and let your lifestyle be the example of what you are inviting men to be a part of.

- Give men what they need in the context of what they want. Most nominally committed men will be focused, at least initially, on their felt needs—career, money, family, time management, and so on. That's okay. Talk to them about money, family, career, time management, and show them what Jesus had to say about these things. In other words, give men what they need in the context of what they want.

- Invest in men who will invest in others. Your men's ministry will grow in proportion to your ability to build not just disciples but disciple-makers. The focus of a men's ministry leader should be to make disciples of men who will in turn disciple others, and so on.

- Create a culture of prayer and love for God's word. A man's life will never change in any significant way apart from the regular study of God's Word and daily prayer.

UMMen Leadership

Certain qualities, skills, and responsibilities are common to all men serving as UMMen leaders.

Personal Traits of a UMMen Leader:
- honest, humble, with a desire to encourage and help others grow as disciples of Jesus Christ
- willing to set aside personal agendas for God's agenda
- growing in his relationship with God through regular prayer, Bible study, and worship attendance
- mature enough to have an orderly life yet flexible enough to consider new and innovative approaches to men's ministry
- practices and models the principles of servant leadership.

Support Traits of a UMMen Leader:
- committed to strengthening United Methodist Men at every level
- works closely with the leadership of the conference, both lay and clergy
- coordinates effectively, as necessary, with other UMM leaders and the GCUMM staff for retreats, events, and other programs
- as an EMS member, models and actively promotes EMS memberships and ministry through Evangelism, Mission, and Spiritual Growth
- has experience and knowledge of the structure and organization of UMMen and the UMC

- willing to answer, through leadership actions, the following questions as they apply to his job level (national, conference, local, etc.): What are the needs of the men in my area of responsibility? What goals and purposes have we established? What will it take to achieve these goals?

Local President

In addition to the universal leader qualities listed, specific responsibilities of the local president include:

Maintaining Annual Charter and EMS Goals
- annual charter renewal
- recruitment of new EMS members
- renewal of lapsed EMS memberships.

Local presidents in coordination with district presidents should determine goals for their local church. An annual report on goals, strategies used to reach goals, and the results of the efforts made should be submitted to the district president. Successful strategies will be compiled and shared with other local UMM presidents.

Encouraging and Equipping Local Church Men
Encourage, train, and help resource all men of the local church. Work with district and local leaders to fill every local UMM vacancy. Recruit and help select local UMM leaders, working in close partnership and cooperation with the local pastor and other local church leaders. Working closely with the district president, the local president should help the men of the local church as needed.

Recruiting Men to Attend Training Events
Ensure that local leaders and men participate in training on a regional or local level. The district president will assist local presidents in planning local training and retreat events.

Providing Local Church UMM Communications
The local church president should be in regular communication with the men of his church as well as the men of the district concerning the plans, goals, programs, and resources available for the men of the church. This can be achieved by regularly contributing to a local church UMM newsletter or submitting regular articles on UMM to the church newspaper. E-mail or fax-based newsletters, and contributions to district laity and clergy newsletters are also recommended. Each local church president should have an annual report ready to present yearly at his charge conference. It is also the local

church president's responsibility to see that United Methodist Men of his church are represented at the district meetings of United Methodist Men. Whenever possible, the local church president should give an oral or written report at appropriate district and local church meetings. Resources for communication pieces may be obtained through the GCUMM staff.

Meeting Regularly with Local Leaders
Local presidents must be intentional in scheduling regular meetings with other local leaders, including pastors, scouting, and prayer/hunger/stewardship advocates. At least twice a year is recommended; once a quarter is preferred.

Supporting and Promoting Attendance at UMM Events
- Promote and recruit attendance at conference, district, and regional events.
- Promote and recruit lay and clergy to attend each quadrennial Congress on United Methodist Men. An attendance goal shall be established for each local church.
- UMM events and programs should be consistent with the purpose and goals of UMMen. Local presidents should review plans for events to ensure they meet this guideline.

Attending Leadership Meetings
Local presidents are expected to attend all meetings called by the district president of United Methodist Men. Local presidents are expected to implement programs approved by the National Association of Conference Presidents, the UMM annual conference leadership team, and the GCUMM. The GCUMM staff will assist local presidents in the implementation of programs.

Maintaining Disciplinary Responsibilities
The local president of United Methodist Men should organize local churchmen of the United Methodist Church according to the *Book of Discipline*. The *Discipline* states that "Each church or charge **shall** [emphasis added] have an organized unit of United Methodist Men chartered and annually renewed through the General Commission on United Methodist Men." It is a primary responsibility of the local president to see that the men of his church are organized and chartered. Selection of the local church president should be accomplished according to the process of selection determined in each local church.

Additional disciplinary responsibilities include:
- working to develop programs relevant to local men
- Encouraging men in daily discipleship including prayer and Scripture
- Promoting the objectives and responsibilities of UMM

- Encouraging and supporting spiritual growth, mission, outreach, prayer, evangelism, and faith development
- Encouraging knowledge and support for the total mission of The United Methodist Church
- Studying and becoming familiar with The United Methodist Church, its organization, doctrine, practices, and beliefs
- Cooperating with all levels of United Methodist Men in achieving goals.

Other Leaders

Every local men's group should elect officers and leaders as necessary to carry out the mission and ministry of United Methodist Men. Elections normally occur in October, with officers assuming duties January 1. Elected officers should attend training events offered within the conference or by the GCUMM. It is recommended that elected leaders contact their district or conference presidents to find out where and when the nearest training event is scheduled.

The leadership team should meet regularly for prayer, planning, and joint discussions of the purpose and plans for mission and ministry among the men of the church in the coming year. The local president should review his job recommendations (page 14) with the other officers, divide responsibilities, and develop strategies concerning the programs and ministries of UMM. Coordination and partnership with the pastor of the local church and the district president of United Methodist Men is important. Establishment of a local constitution and bylaws is recommended. Sample constitutions and bylaws may be obtained from the national office of the GCUMM. Tenure of officers is normally determined in the bylaws for all leadership positions.

The Nominating Committee

A nominating committee should be composed of local United Methodist Men whose purpose is to nominate to the membership the officers of the local unit. The nomination of the president should be done prayerfully with the local president job description used for determining who might best fit the position. The president should be a member in good standing with the local church. It is recommended that input be solicited from the pastor of the church on the potential UMM president before the nominee is asked to consider serving in the position. The nominating committee may include three to five men elected from the membership of the unit. They have the responsibility to seek out men to fill vacancies between elections as well as at normal election times.

The president of the local unit will provide the following information to the chairman of the nominating committee:

- *Men's Ministries,* Guidelines for Leading Your Congregation (this Guideline)
- constitution and bylaws of the unit (if you have not yet developed them, sample constitution and bylaws along with instructions can be obtained through the GCUMM office or see gcumm.org Web site).
- mission and purpose statement (see pages 6-7)
- a list of male members of the church and current leadership, including the number of years each has served
- *UM Men Ministry Program Book* (ordered through GCUMM office)
- information about upcoming training events (obtained through the UMM district president).

Leader Traits

As the nominating committee conducts its work, personal contacts are important. Experience on the part of the candidate is always helpful but should not limit the search. Enthusiasm, energy, vision, and commitment to Christ are critical factors in the selection of all United Methodist Men leaders. Other criteria that should be considered when looking for leaders include:

- good communication skills—leaders must be able to communicate effectively.
- availability—leadership should be available for meetings, ministry, prayer, and planning. A capable person who becomes a leader but is too busy with other things cannot be effective.
- supportive of the ministries of the local church—UMM leaders should always work in cooperation and partnership with the pastor and other local church ministries.
- willing to enthusiastically promote UMM ministries—Effective leaders work together at all levels to build a strong and successful men's ministry.
- an EMS member—all leaders should be EMS members (see page 25) because they are asked to promote EMS to all the men of the church.
- good relational skills—leaders should be able to relate to all the men of the church, have sound temperament, and exhibit the fruit of the spirit (Galatians 5:22-26).

The chair of the nominating committee has the responsibility for submitting the committee recommendations to the unit. Election of officers may be by voice vote or ballot. Bylaws should state the percentage of votes needed for election. Names and addresses of elected officers should be submitted with the renewal charter application.

Responsibilities of Local Officers

Every men's ministry unit in the local church needs elected leaders for the proper working and effective mission and ministry of the local UMM unit.

President
The president should be informed about the nature, scope, and criteria for successful men's ministry. The president and other officers should review the current *UMMen Program Book,* available through the national office of the GCUMM. Officers should also be familiar with the *Book of Discipline* and *The Book of Resolutions of the United Methodist Church.* Additionally, the president should be an EMS member who regularly reads the *UMMen Magazine* for information, inspiration, and ideas. (See job description on pages 14-16.)

The president should be in frequent dialogue with the men of his church to assess their needs, receive suggestions, and maximize the impact of men's ministry. The president should be an advocate for all the ministries of the church, the pastor and staff, and the mission work of UMM. He should encourage all men of the church to attend district and conference UMM events and bring as many men as possible to the quadrennial National Gathering of United Methodist Men (formerly called Congress).

The UMM local president is also a member of the local church council or equivalent and is usually a member of the local church charge conference (where he may be asked to submit a written or oral report).

Vice President
The vice president acts in the absence of the president when necessary. The vice president may be assigned responsibilities as deemed necessary by the president and executive committee. The vice president is expected to be well informed about United Methodist Men's activities, mission, and ministries. He works closely with the president in interpreting and advocating United Methodist Men. Local constitutions and bylaws may identify specific responsibilities of the vice president. He shall be an EMS member and a voting member of the executive committee.

Secretary
The secretary of the local UMM unit shall be responsible for keeping records of business meetings, executive committee meetings, correspondence, and other responsibilities that may be assigned by the local constitution or bylaws. He should be an EMS member and is a voting member of the executive committee.

Treasurer
The treasurer of the local UMM unit shall have the responsibility of collecting and distributing all funds. He shall maintain good records and provide regular reports to the executive committee concerning the income, expenses,

and distribution of all funds of the local UMM unit. Disbursement of funds not authorized through the annual budget can only be made after consultation with the president or executive committee or by direction of the local unit as a whole. The treasurer is responsible for seeing that the annual charter renewal fee is paid in a timely manner. He may also help develop the annual budget for the local unit. He should be an EMS member.

Executive Committee
The executive committee of the local UMM unit shall be composed of the elected officers, any committee chairs, and other leaders as may be designated by the local constitution and bylaws. Any district, conference, jurisdictional, or nationally elected leader of United Methodist Men is a member of the local unit and may serve on the executive committee. The executive committee serves as a leadership team working in partnership with the pastor and other local church leaders. Together, they pray, plan, and carry out the mission and ministry of the local church and men's ministry. The executive committee manages the business of the local unit, reporting its activities at least annually. It is recommended that most business decisions and discussions be made at special business meetings open to all interested persons. Business discussions should be avoided or minimized at UMM gatherings, events, mission work, or ministry activities.

Guidelines for UMM Meetings

United Methodist Men are most effective when they offer a variety of programs and ministry opportunities to the men of the church. It is crucial that the time invested by men result in a quality experience that enriches and equips them as servant leaders in MENistry. Without well planned, helpful, interesting, and spiritually challenging meetings and programs, men will avoid or drop out of regular participation in the local unit.

Here are some additional ideas for building effective men's ministry in your local church:
- Be flexible on meeting or program times and locations. Determine the times and places that fit the needs of the majority of men, including younger men. It is impossible to meet everyone's needs all the time, but flexibility allows you to avoid "doing the same thing, the same way, at the same times and locations as we have always done it."
- Encourage men to meet in smaller groups that fit their needs. Young men may want to meet over breakfast at a restaurant once a week. Some men may want to meet for a bag lunch downtown every other week. Some men like the monthly meeting at the church with a meal. Assume that men's

needs and interests are varied. Help them to form groups around common interests and to meet at their convenience. General meetings for all men can take place less frequently or at special events.
- Provide inspirational music, speakers, and programs at general membership gatherings. Infrequent inspirational programs keep men interested and involved more than frequent routine business-like meetings.
- Use resources provided by the national office for programs, training, spiritual growth, and mission opportunities. The national office offers program materials and ideas for spiritually centered programs and events.
- Start on time and end on time. Do not allow meetings to drag beyond the announced ending time. If things do run on, invite men who need to leave to depart at the scheduled end time.
- Publicize effectively. Encourage men to personally invite men who have never attended, especially younger men and sons. Provide funds for men who need help with the cost.
- Equip your pastors by sponsoring their participation at as many UMM events as possible and by providing men's ministry resources to them. Pay for your pastor's EMS membership.
- Involve as many men as possible as volunteers in any UMM activity. Some men are more likely to attend if they are asked to help than if they are simply "invited." More men who help will feel "ownership" in the event.

The Charter

The *Book of Discipline* states that every men's organization in the local church shall have an official charter through the General Commission on United Methodist Men. UMM charters recognize the connectional nature of men's ministry in the United Methodist Church. Charters and annual recertification help to strengthen the local and national connectional community ties of UMM. It was recognized that although men could conduct local church men's ministries, there was a need for a national organization that would provide resources, training, information, and inspiration to help make local men's ministries more effective.

The national office of the General Commission on United Methodist Men provides services for local units, subdistricts, districts, conferences, and jurisdictional organizations of United Methodist Men. Affiliate organizations related to the GCUMM include: the National Association of Conference Presidents; the United Methodist Men Foundation; the National Association of United Methodist Scouters; the World Fellowship of Methodist and Uniting Church Men; the National Coalition of Men's

Ministries; the North American Conference of Church Men's Staff; National Fatherhood Initiative; the Boy Scouts of America, Girl Scouts of the U.S.A., Camp Fire U.S.A., and 4-H.

The General Commission on United Methodist Men oversees and manages the mission and ministries of United Methodist Men on a national scale. The GCUMM conducts training opportunities annually for conference and district presidents. Jurisdictional training events are also offered for local presidents and other interested leaders in men's ministries.

It is the responsibility of the GCUMM to conduct and manage the quadrennial National Gathering of United Methodist Men. The next National Gathering (formerly called Congress on Men) will be held at Purdue University in West Lafayette, Indiana, on July 15-17, 2005. Contact GCUMM for additional information or go to the GCUMM Web site (www.gcumm.org).

The GCUMM represents United Methodist Men's interests in other general agencies of the church as well as with the central conferences of the United Methodist Church.

Chartered United Methodist Men's Units Receive:

- *UMMen Magazine.* The official magazine of and for United Methodist Men containing informational and inspirational articles designed to help men become servant leaders. This magazine features *MensNews*, the official UMM newsletter containing news, ideas, announcements, and recognition of what is happening among UMMen around the world. Also contained in the newsletter is information about scouting ministry, the UMM Foundation, and missions. It is published four times a year.
- United Methodist Men's Membership Cards. Enough membership cards for all the men in your local unit.
- Frameable Charter Certificate. Quadrennial certificate with yearly renewal stickers provides an attractive affirmation of the local UMM unit.
- Important information critical to conducting effective men's ministry. Charters come with a packet full of vital information important to successful UMM units.

A first-time charter may choose to prorate the charter fee for the first year on a quarterly basis as follows:

Jan.-March	$65.00
April-June	$48.75
July-Sept.	$32.50

Example: A new charter sent to GCUMM on May 1 would include a check for $48.75.

- *Program Book.* Each chartered unit receives a program and ministry idea book designed to help you with ideas for programs and ministries for your local unit.
- UMMen *Tacklebox.* Resource catalog designed to offer local units books, tapes, videos, training and study materials, pens, shirts, and other important resources for effective men's ministry in the local church.
- Upper Room Prayer Line. Information about the Upper Room Prayer Line sponsored by United Methodist Men.
- Missions. Information about the nationally sponsored UMM mission opportunities.
- Assistance with program planning.
- Web site information. Information about the official United Methodist Men's Web site (www.gcumm.org)

Building Interest for Chartering

There is no secret formula for organizing a successful United Methodist Men's unit. It does not happen overnight. First, get the support of your pastor. Success is dependent upon his or her enthusiastic support. Arrange a time for a meeting, and include your pastor and several men from your congregation. Invite your district United Methodist Men's president. At this meeting, make plans for the steps you will follow to form a United Methodist Men's unit.

Your Plans Should Include These Steps:
- Discuss the purpose of United Methodist Men as stated in the *Book of Discipline*. Read the information in *Men's Ministries,* Guidelines for Leading Your Congregation 2005-2008.
- Develop a plan for publicity and recruiting members. Set a date for the organizational meeting.
- At the organizational meeting select the officers. Set the date for the monthly meeting. Prepare a constitution and bylaws for your unit.
- Use some of the many aids available to help get off to a good start. They include *Men's Ministries,* Guidelines for Leading Your Congregation 2005-2008 and *Program Book.* The *MensNews* featured in the *UMMen Magazine* is a publication for presidents, secretaries, and other men who subscribe through the Every Man Shares through Evangelism, Mission & Spiritual Life (EMS) program. Write the General Commission on United Methodist Men, P.O. Box 340006, Nashville, TN 37203-0006, for brochures and additional information.
- Charter your unit. It is important to charter. After the initial charter, units

should be renewed annually. Some ask, "Why should we charter as long as we have a men's group and meet regularly?" There are several reasons why it would be helpful for you to charter. Most important, your men become a link in the international movement of men extending the kingdom of God. Your charter gift supports missions that one unit alone can't do. They include the Living Prayer Center, Civic Youth Serving Agencies/Scouting, and the exciting Men in Mission emphasis. Your charter fee provides training for officers and programs designed for men. Chartering is a base from which to reach out in mission through the effort of thousands of men's groups.

Important Functions of the Annual Charter and Annual Renewal are to:

- update and correct the mailing addresses of current officers so that the proper leaders receive the current information
- link men's units around the world for common mission and ministry support
- provide support for the development of resources especially designed for men; mission opportunities sponsored by UMM; and evangelism emphasis of men, youth, and scouting ministries sponsored by UMM.

How to Charter:

1. List the church name, address, city, state, and zip (plus four if known).
2. Give your pastor's name and phone number, United Methodist church national code if known, district and conference name.
3. Give the president's name, address, city, state, zip (plus four if known), and phone number.
4. Give the treasurer's name, address, city, state, zip (plus four if known), and phone number.
5. Have the treasurer prepare a check for $65.
6. Mail the check and the above information to United Methodist Men, P.O. Box 440515, Nashville, TN 37244-0515.

For annual recertification, churches and presidents are mailed notices with a return envelope and the certification information in the fall.

UNITED METHODIST MEN CHARTER APPLICATION
THE UNITED METHODIST CHURCH
"BE YE DOERS OF THE WORD AND NOT HEARERS ONLY"

The General Commission on United Methodist Men is an official church organization recognized by the General Conference. The men's organization gains strength, mission outreach, program information, and visibility because of the general church recognition of United Methodist Men.

ANNUAL CHARTER RECERTIFICATION

How to charter or recertify:
✓ Complete the information needed below.
✓ Have treasurer prepare a check for $65.00 for a contribution to the mission of United Methodist Men.
✓ Mail this form with your check to:

General Commission on United Methodist Men
P.O. Box 440515
Nashville, TN 37244-0515
(615) 340-7148, Fax (615) 340-1770

FOR OFFICE USE ONLY
Check Amt.:_____
Check No._____
Date_____
Initials_____
ID#_____
JAD_____
Entry Date_____
Initials_____

***We can charter jointly 2 or more units as one, if they are meeting together.

PLEASE CHECK ONE:
❏ This is an application for a NEW CHARTER
❏ This is an application for ANNUAL RECERTIFICATION OF CHARTER
❏ This is a recertification for a LAPSED CHARTER

UM CHURCH CODE (IF KNOWN): _____

CHURCH _____
(OR THE NAME OF YOUR UNIT, FELLOWSHIP OR GROUP)

_____
STREET ADDRESS

_____
CITY, STATE, ZIP

PASTOR _____ PHONE _____

CONFERENCE _____ DISTRICT _____

PRESIDENT _____ PHONE _____
NAME

_____
STREET ADDRESS

_____ _____
CITY, STATE, ZIP   E mail

CHARTER SECRETARY _____ PHONE _____
                        NAME

_____
STREET ADDRESS

_____ _____
CITY, STATE, ZIP   E mail

24 Guidelines for Leading Your Congregation

The EMS Program

The General Commission on United Methodist Men encourages every man in The United Methodist Church to invest in its EMS Program. Every Man Shares in Evangelism, Mission, and Spiritual Life is an annual UMM membership that supports the ministry and work of the United Methodist Men worldwide. The EMS program enables UMMen to acquire, develop, and distribute quality materials, programs, and resources for UMMen. These tools help men effectively accomplish evangelism, mission, and spiritual life. We equip men individually, in small teams, and charter units for Kingdom work, as they support their pastors and local congregations more effectively.

Benefits of your EMS Membership...
* *UMMen Magazine* (which includes newsletter)
* Devotional Book
* *Tacklebox* Discounts
* Complimentary UMMen Novelties
* Supports Worldwide UMMen Missions and Ministries
* Discounts on UMMen events

Where Does the Money Go?
* $5.00 to Conference and District support of UMM Ministries
* $.75 to Jurisdiction support of UMM Ministries
* $.75 to National Association of Conference Presidents to support UMM Ministries
* $1.50 to Scouting and Civic Youth Ministries
* $.75 to support UMM Missions
* $.75 to support the Upper Room Prayer Ministry
* $15.00 to direct expenses related to training, production of resources, *UMMen Magazine,* postage, etc.
* $5.50 to administrative expense for EMS Ministry

Yes! I will invest in Evangelism, Mission, and Spiritual Life.
My $30 is enclosed: ❑ Check   ❑ Money Order
❑ Renewal Subscriber   ❑ First-time Subscriber

Name _____ Church _____
Address _____ Address _____
City, State, Zip _____ City, State, Zip _____
Home Phone _____ District & Conference _____
E-mail _____

Mail to:
General Commission on United Methodist Men
P.O. Box 440515
Nashville, TN 37244-0515

GENERAL COMMISSION ON UNITED METHODIST MEN

UMMen Resources

It is the desire of the General Commission on United Methodist Men to provide the best quality resources to the men of the United Methodist Church. Books, magazines, newsletters, videotapes, and other printed resources are available to help men become Servant Leaders of Jesus Christ.

UMMen Magazine is a quarterly publication that addresses the spiritual issues facing the United Methodist man, his family, his ministry, and his world. A special feature of this magazine is the *MensNews,* which highlights local men's ministry worldwide.

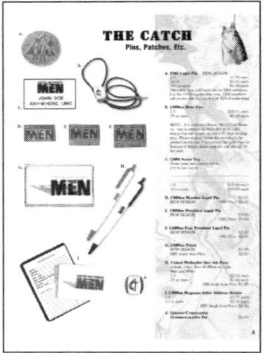

Tacklebox is our companion catalog for UMMen resources and specialty items. Shirts, hats, pens, brochures, and other novelty items can be ordered from this catalog.

In addition to these resources, we annually publish the *UMMen Ministry Program Book,* which is a practical workbook for men to build (from scratch if necessary) an effective men's ministry in a local congregation.

Please contact us if you have any questions or would like to order any UMMen resources.

General Commission on United Methodist Men
P.O. Box 340006
Nashville, TN 37203-0006
(615) 340-7145

The Society of St. Andrew, Meals for Millions, and the Hunger Relief Advocate Initiative

Meals for Millions is the primary anti-hunger mission of United Methodist Men. Established in 1986 as an Advance Special Mission Project of the United Methodist Church (#982225-8), *Meals for Millions* is designed to get United Methodist Men directly involved in leading our church to fight hunger in proven, cost effective ways through the ministries of the Society of St. Andrew. Through *Meals for Millions*, UMMen can literally feed millions of people in the name of Christ, take a leadership position in all levels of the church in fighting hunger, and become involved in hands-on ministry to the poor.

The Society of St. Andrew is a nonprofit, ecumenical Christian ministry dedicated to fighting domestic hunger. Founded in 1979 by two United Methodist pastors, it is also an Advance Special mission project of the UMC. The Society saves fresh produce that would otherwise go to waste and delivers it to people in need. Through the Society of St. Andrew's *Potato Project*, fifteen to twenty-five million pounds of produce—primarily potatoes—are saved annually to provide forty-five to seventy-five million servings of food to food banks, soup kitchens, Native American reservations, and other distribution agencies for free. The Society's *Harvest of Hope* and *Gleaning Network* programs also annually save more than twenty million pounds of food from farmers' fields and deliver it to the nation's hungry.

In 1998, the General Commission on United Methodist Men and the National Association of Conference Presidents joined with the Society of St. Andrew in the *Hunger Relief Advocate Initiative*. This joint effort is designed to help the United Methodist Church engage in ministry with the poor and hungry under leadership of United Methodist Men. Hunger Relief Advocates (HRAs) are charged with: establishing and administering gleaning networks to provide food directly to those in need locally; raising awareness of the extent of hunger in America and training in the development of local anti-hunger programs; championing UMMen participation in the *Meals for Millions* program; serving as an education and action resource for hunger relief and poverty issues; and involvement in other hunger relief activities. The ultimate goal of the *Hunger Relief Advocate Initiative* is to feed America's hungry through the work of part-time HRAs in every annual conference plus volunteer advocates in each UMMen district and each local UMMen's group. In addition, the *HRA Initiative* seeks to increase direct hunger relief through the *Potato Project*.

The *HRA Initiative* is funded through UMMen *Meals for Millions* contributions. Every UMMen fellowship is asked to become a Challenge Fellowship by donating a minimum of $200 annually to *Meals for Millions*. These donations go exclusively to the *HRA Initiative*, and each Challenge Fellowship provides more than 20,000 servings of food to hungry Americans in the name of Jesus Christ. Additionally, individuals are invited to become Challenge Disciples by donating at least $25 to *Meals for Millions* twice annually in response to call letters. Through their donations, every Challenge Disciple provides about 5,000 servings of food annually to their hungry neighbors.

Join UMMen across the country and get involved today in the fight against hunger! Together, we can literally *"give them something to eat"* by providing Meals for Millions! For free brochures and additional information call or write the GCUMM office (615-340-7145), or contact the Society of St. Andrew: 3383 Sweet Hollow Road, Big Island, VA 24526; 800-333-4597; email: sosahra@endhunger.org Web sites: www.endhunger.org; www.gbgm-umc.org/mfm.

UMMen Ministry Survey

Background Information
1. Age: ❏ 18-24 ❏ 25-29 ❏ 30-39 ❏ 40-49 ❏ 50-64 ❏ 65+
2. Marital Status: ❏ Single ❏ Married
   Number of Children?_____
3. Type of work _____
4. Which of these issues are most important to you? (check two most important)
   ❏ Finding a job   ❏ Male roles and identity   ❏ Retirement
   ❏ Relationship   ❏ Work, home, ministry   ❏ Reaching other
     to wife   men
   ❏ Job security   ❏ Parenting skills   ❏ Spiritual life

A Man and His Family
5. Would you be interested in a monthly meeting on family issues? (parenting, etc.) ❏ Yes ❏ No
6. When would be the best time for you to attend this meeting?
   ❏ Saturday morning   ❏ Weeknight   ❏ Sunday night
   ❏ Sunday morning   ❏ _____

7. What family topics would you like to see addressed?
   ❏ Keep romance alive   ❏ Being spiritual leader   ❏ Communicating
   ❏ Disciplining children ❏ Handling conflict   with wife
   ❏ Other_____

Men in the Marketplace
8. How can we best help you integrate your Christian faith into your job?
   ❏ Monthly meeting with speaker
   ❏ 3-5 week seminar on ethics, job issues, etc.
   ❏ Small group meetings to discuss issues

9. Best time for these small group seminars?
   ❏ Weekday morning   ❏ Saturday morning
   ❏ Weekday evening   ❏ Sunday night

10. Topics I would like to hear addressed (check top 3)
    ❏ Handling stress   ❏ Coping with failure
    ❏ Sharing faith w/ co-workers ❏ Changing careers
    ❏ Planning retirement   ❏ (Avoiding success obsession
    ❏ Relationships on the job   ❏ Mentoring
    ❏ Remaining ethically sharp

Men in the Mission
11. Would a short-term mission trip be of interest to you? ❑ Yes ❑ No
12. What type of short-term missions trip would interest you the most?
    ❑ Construction project ❑ Business trip
    ❑ Medical trip ❑ Athletic trip

13. What would be a good length of stay for such a trip?_____

Retreats
14. If we would begin to have retreats as part of the ministry, would you be interested? Y N
15. What type of retreat would interest you most?
    ❑ Teaching Type ❑ Spiritual and personal renewal
    ❑ Adventure type (canoeing, fishing, etc.)
    ❑ Networking with other men

16. How long should the retreat be? ❑ one night ❑ two nights
17. How far would you drive for a retreat? ❑ ½ hour ❑ 1 hour
    ❑ more than 1 hour

Man-to-Man
18. Are you currently attending a men's Bible study group? ❑ Yes ❑ No
19. If not, would you be interested in attending a men's small group?
    ❑ Yes ❑ No
20. What would you like to see happen in that group? (check two)
    ❑ Study the Bible ❑ Pray for one another
    ❑ Talk about problems at home and work
    ❑ Integrate your faith with your life

21. Which would you prefer for meeting?
    ❑ Every week for an hour ❑ Once a month for 3 hours
    ❑ Every other week

22. When would you prefer to meet?
    ❑ Early morning ❑ During lunch ❑ After work ❑ Over weekend

Men's Conference
23. What type of seminars would you like to see at the Men's Conference? (check three)
    ❑ Parenting ❑ Work ethics ❑ Balancing work, home, ministry
    ❑ Masculinity ❑ Finances ❑ Changing jobs or retirement
    ❑ Relationship to wife ❑ Growing as a Christian ❑ Evangelism

Men's Ministry

24. Would you be willing to assist in Men's Ministry? ❑ Yes ❑ No
25. If yes, what are your areas of potential interest?
    ❑ Publicity　　　　❑ Lead small group　　❑ Marketplace Ministries
    ❑ Organize events ❑ Telephoning　　　　❑ Teach Bible study
    ❑ Work in kitchen ❑ Work projects　　　❑ Evangelism

26. What do you or would you personally like to accomplish through your involvement in Men's Ministry? (check two)
    ❑ A closer walk with God
    ❑ An outlet to vent problems or frustrations
    ❑ Fellowship with other Christian men
    ❑ More involvement in the church
    ❑ A chance to meet other men
    ❑ (Other (please specify) _____

When the entire men's program is determined, I would like someone to contact me so I can become more involved or receive more information. Y N
❑ Yes ❑ No

If yes, Name_____
Address, City, State, Zip _____
_____
Phone (w), (h) _____
e-mail address _____

In the space below, please list additional comments about the Men's Ministry that you may have. You may optionally include your name, address, phone, etc. Thank you very much for completing this survey.

Resources

- *UMMen Magazine*—provides inspiration and information for men. View archived back issues at www.gcumm.org
- *Power Tools*—an electronic resource that provides tips for developing effective men's ministry. Produced monthly. Available at www.gcumm.org
- *Messages for Men*—an electronic resource that offers a reflection on key men's issues contained in one of the lectionary passages for the month with discussion questions; produced monthly. Available at gcumm.org.
- *TQuest for Men*—a journey for men in small teams, utilizing men's spiritual formation resources. To download a free sample go to: www.tquestformen.com
- *Man in the Mirror Weekly* Briefing an e-mail resource to equip, encourage and challenge men's ministry leaders. Available at www.maninthemirror.org
- *Dad e-mail*. An e-mail resource through National Fatherhood Initiative that provides news and information relevant to fatherhood issues as well as regular updates of NFI events, conferences, and fatherhood forums. Available at www.fatherhood.org
- *Fathers.com* a weekly e-mail that covers a timely fathering topic and provides practical fathering tips. Available at www.fathers.com
- *Hope's Gift International Daily E-Mail Devotionals* designed for men in the marketplace. Available at www.eprayerconnect.org
- *Champions for Christ* a program that connects men relationally with boys and young men from female single-parent homes. Contact: Rev. Jim Hollis, Proactive Evangelism Ministries (770) 949-9764 www.proactive-evangelism.org
- *A Chosen Generation* an ecumenical ministry that promotes the passage of boys and girls into Christian adulthood. This program engages the entire congregation in this process. Contact: Rev. Chuck Stecker, (303) 948-1112 www.achosengeneration.org
- *National Hunger Relief Advocate* find out about hunger relief and food recovery opportunities. Contact Del Ketcham (615) 340 7125 hratn@endhunger.org
- *Scouting and Youth Serving Agencies* find out how to reach boys and girls through Boy Scouts of America, Girl Scouts of the U.S.A., 4-H and Camp Fire U.S.A.. Contact: Larry Coppock (615) 340 7149